Photographs
Of
Western Massachusetts

JOHN C. POWER

Places and things around the Pioneer Valley

GEORGE M. POWER

He saw ordinary things in an extraordinary way

'CHOCOLATE THE HORSE'
Goshen, Massachusetts
John C. Power

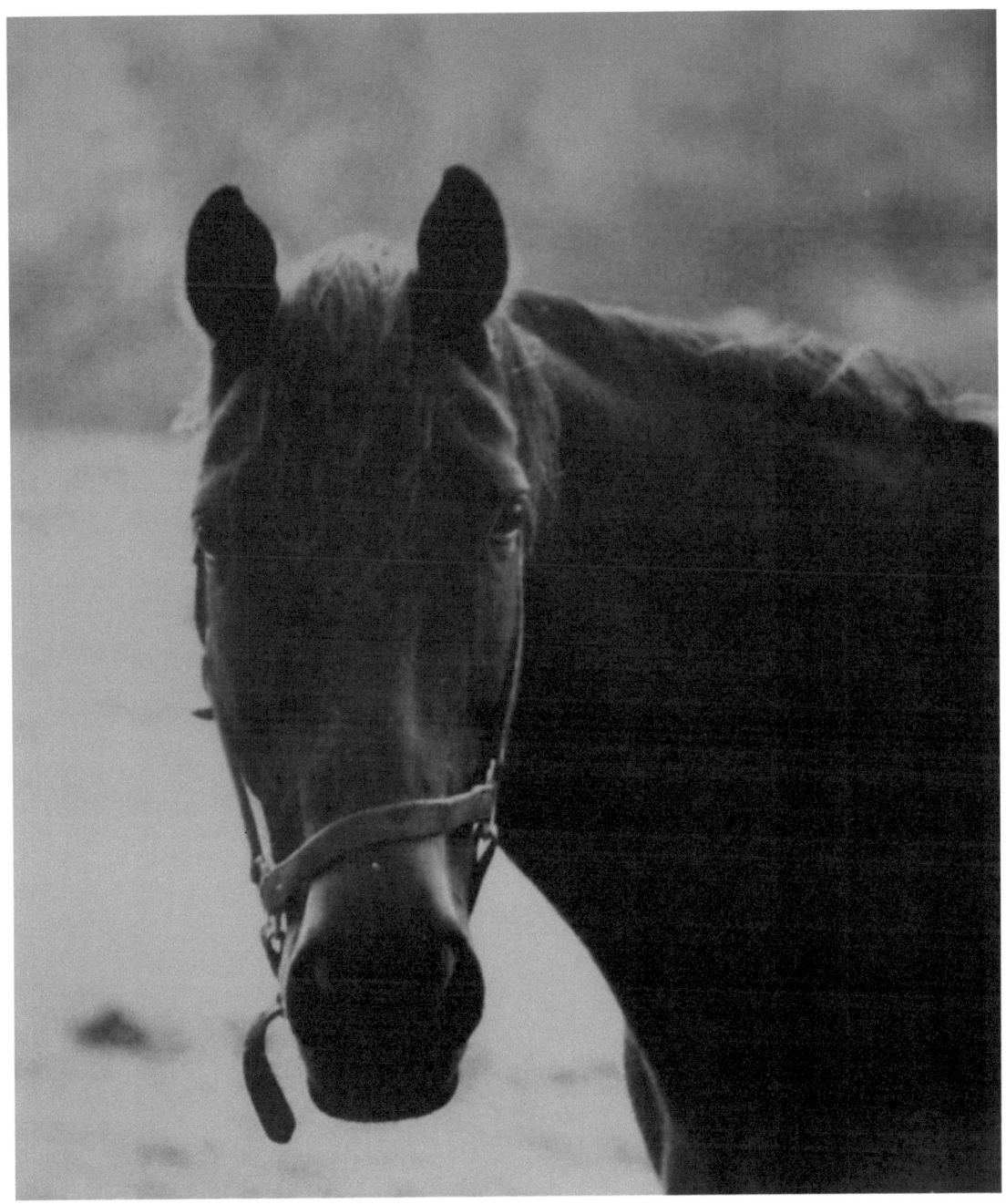

Out for a ride in the hill towns, I came across Chocolate. He was very friendly and was eager to have his picture taken. Unfortunately I didn't have any treats to give him in return.

'PIANO KEYS'
At Home
Amherst, Massachusetts
John C. Power

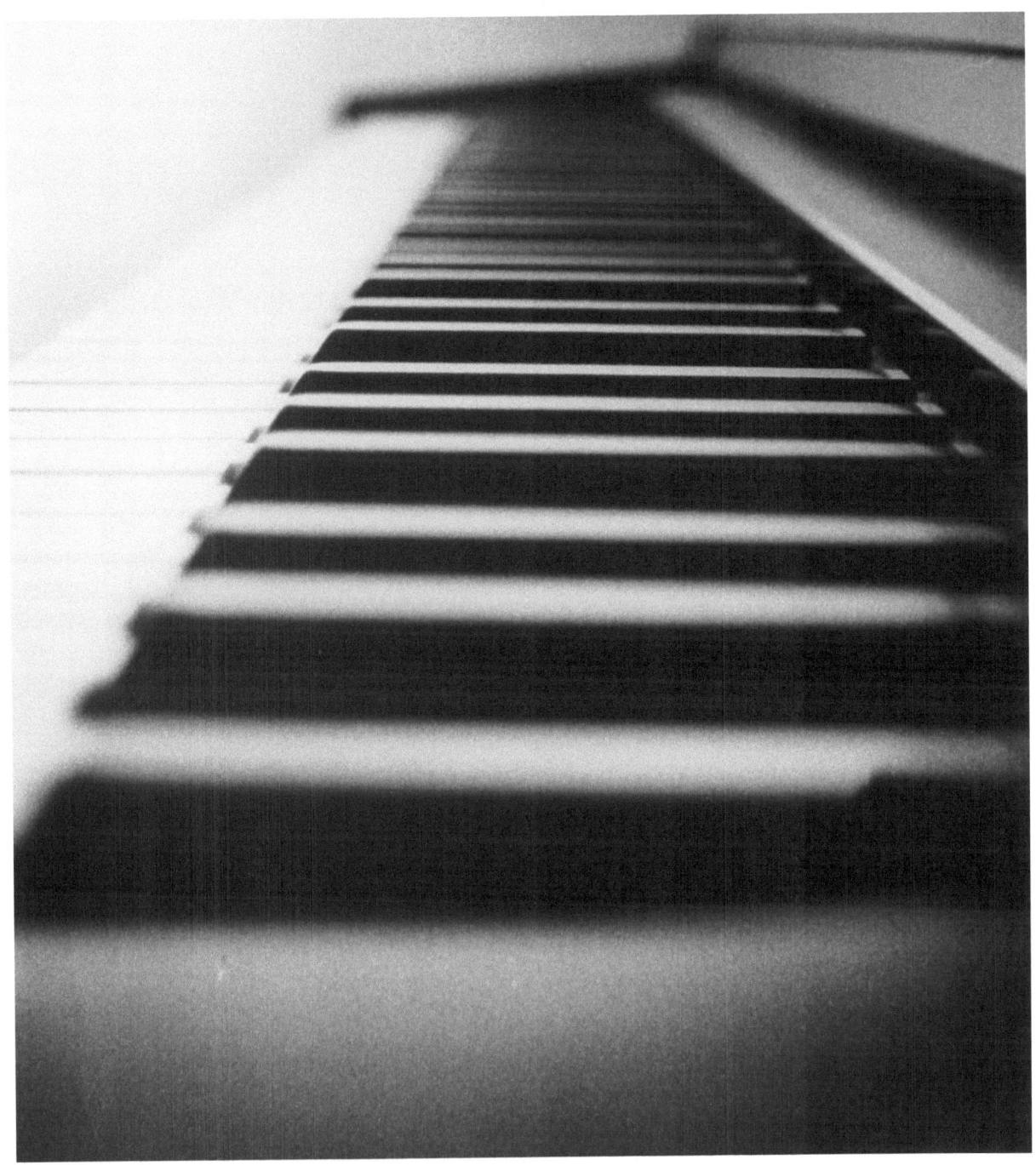

I thought this made for an interesting photo on black and white film. The depth of field gives the effect of out of focus, in focus, then out again. The piano belonged to a friend and former roommate of mine. He's an excellent musician.

'IN THE WOODS'
Amherst, Massachusetts
John C. Power

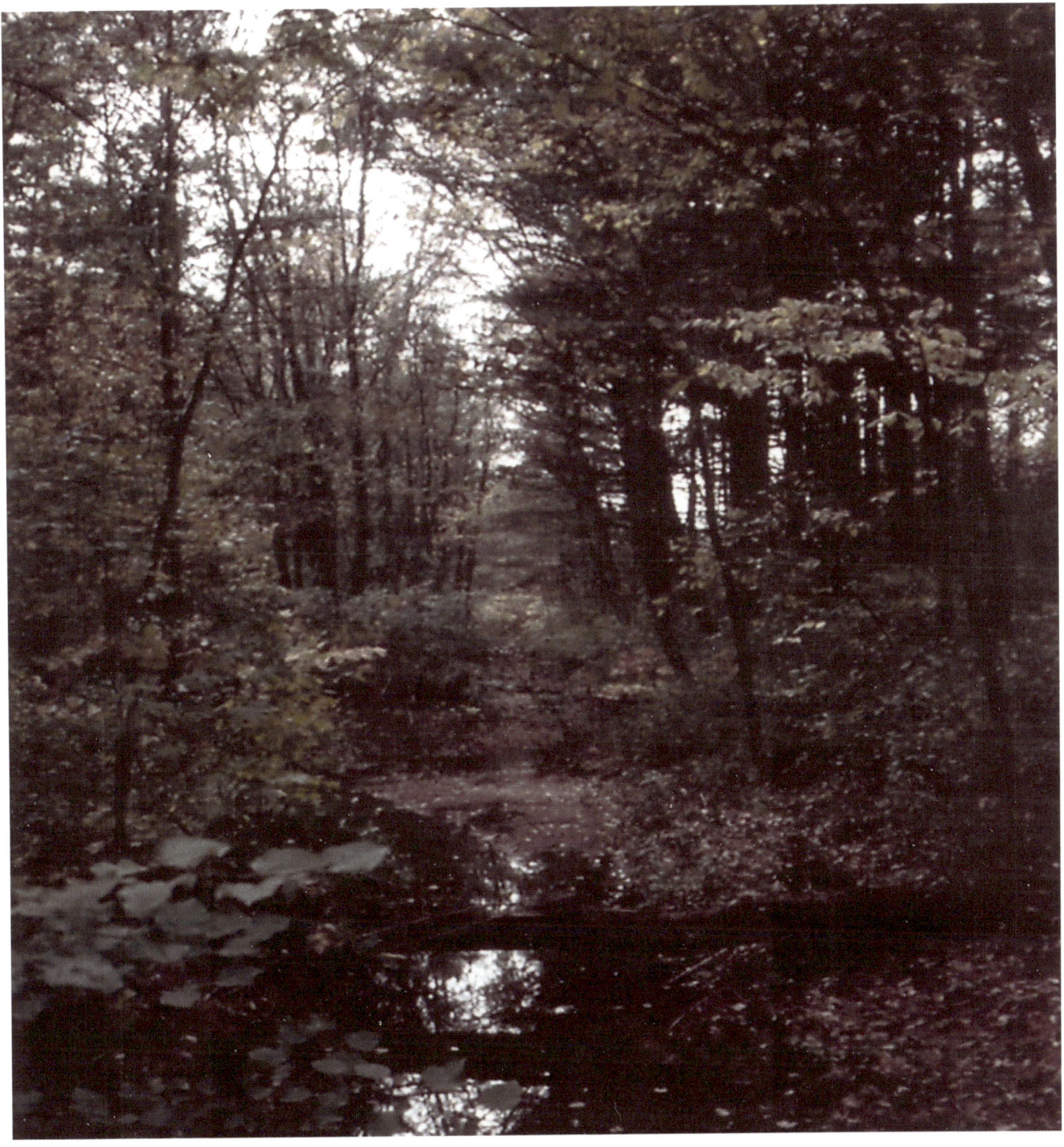

This is a popular hiking trail here in Amherst. After a brief bit of rain I went for a walk and shot what was in front of me. I liked the effect of the puddles along with the leaves on the ground.

‘AUTUMN COLORS’
Easthampton, Massachusetts
John C. Power

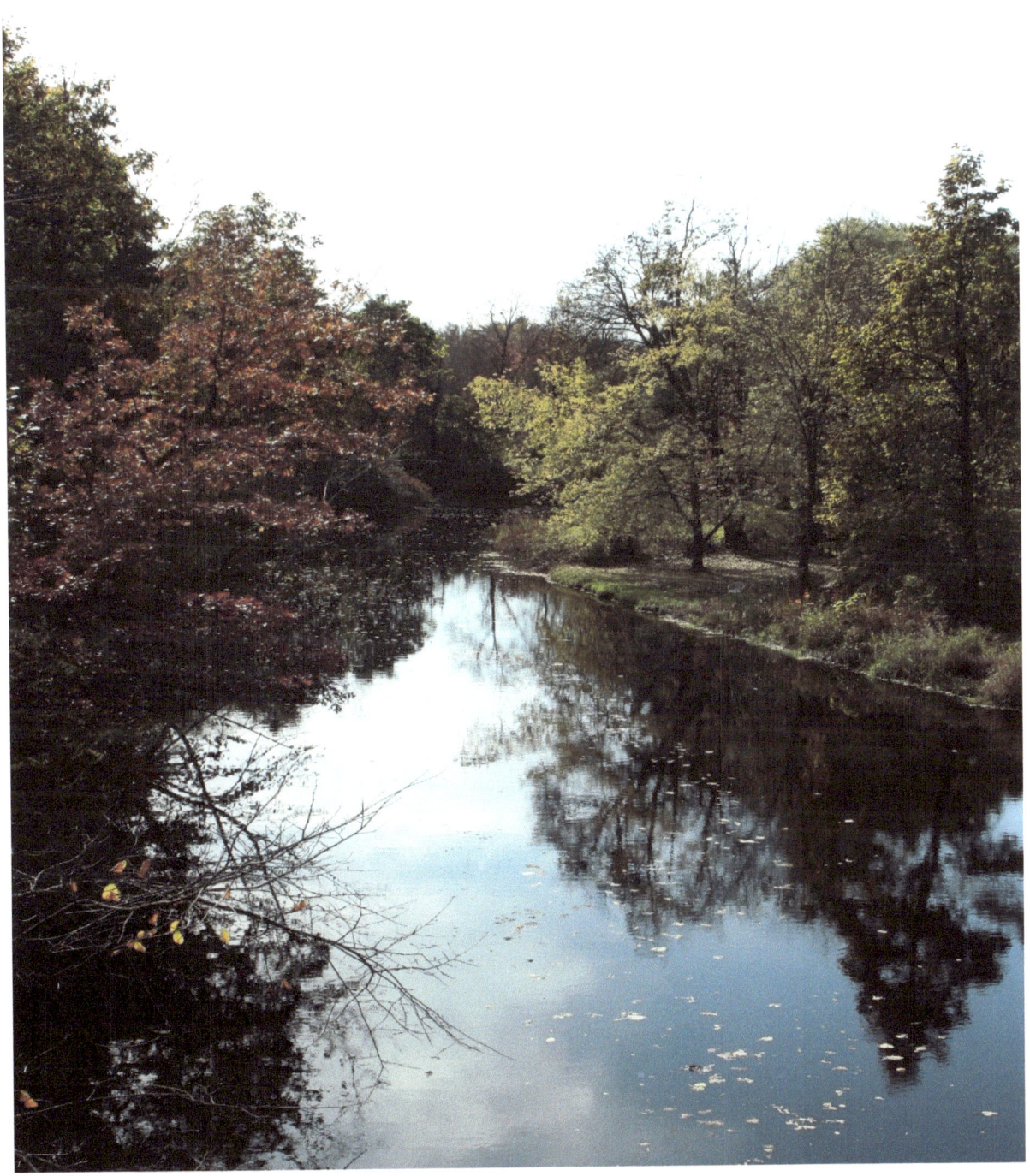

The fall colors made for a nice reflection in the river underneath the bridge on Rt. 10 in Easthampton. This photo is still among one of my favorite peaceful scenes.

'MILL RIVER'
Leeds, Massachusetts
John C. Power

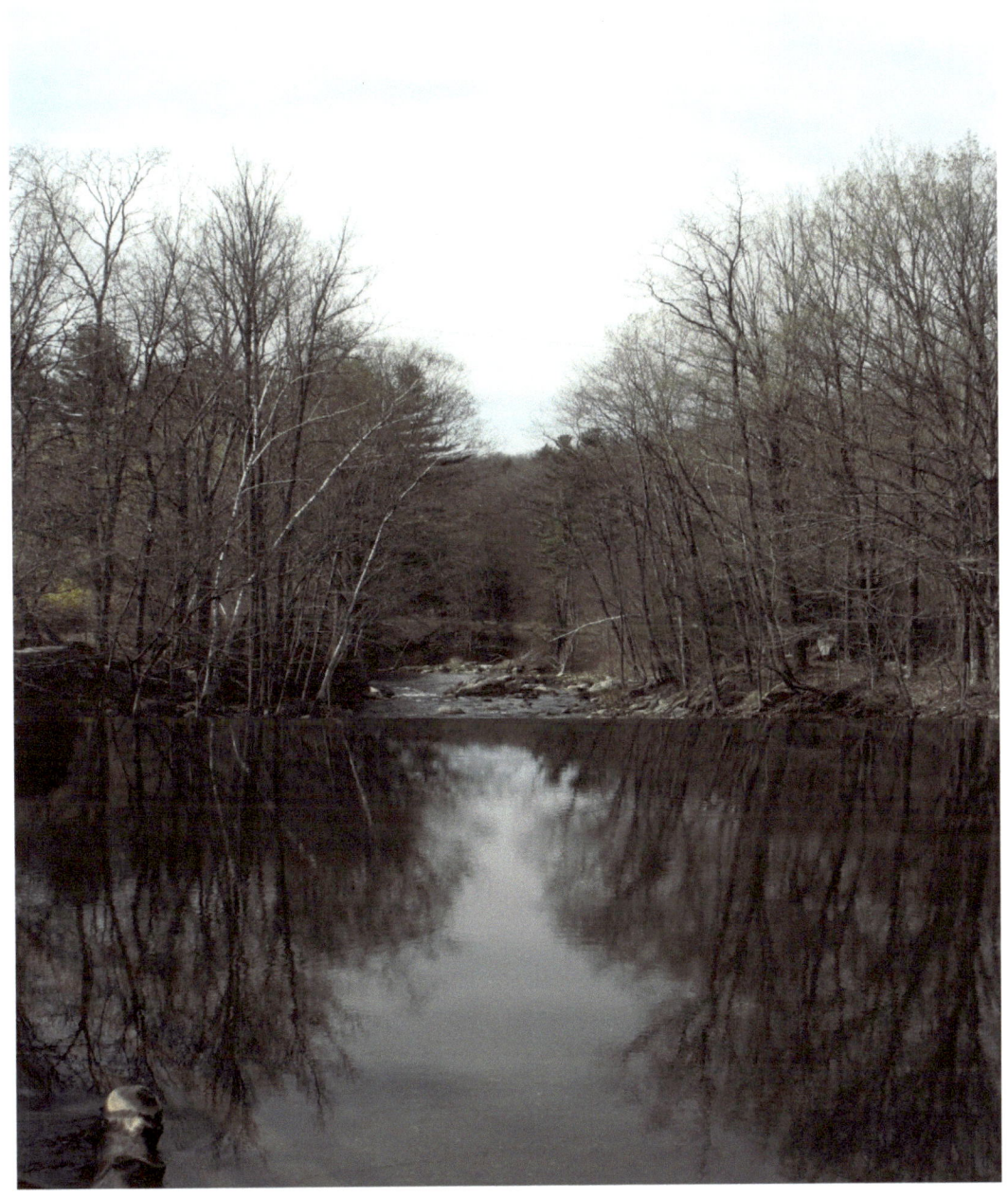

The Mill River in Leeds was right down the street from my parent's house. My father and I used to come here a lot and take pictures. At one time this river powered local mills in the area.

'MORNING LIGHT'
At Home
Amherst, Massachusetts
John C. Power

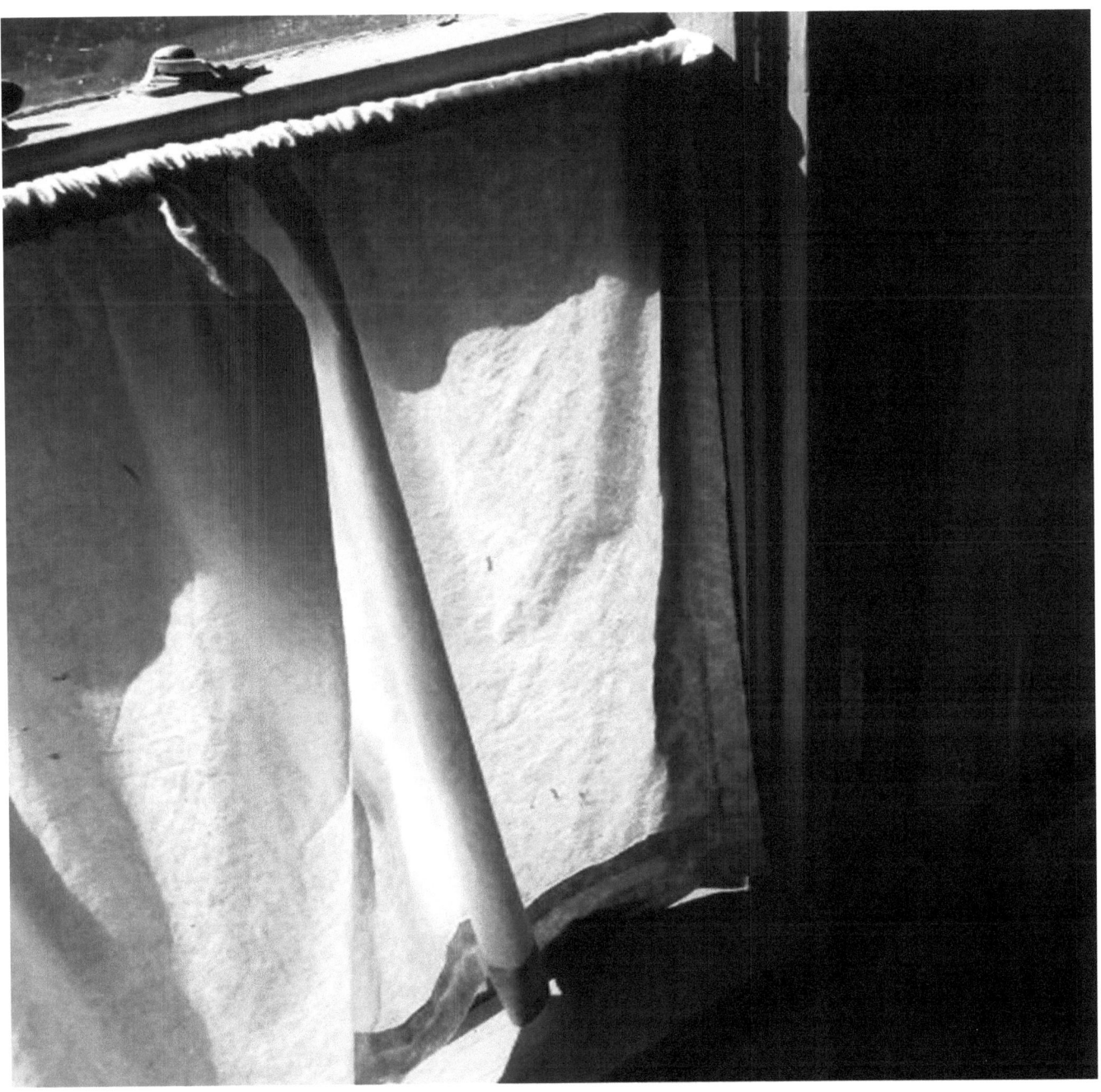

Early morning light at the break of day illuminates through the curtain creating a soft effect.
It's the perfect time to take a photograph.

'RAIN DROPS'
At Home
Amherst, Massachusetts
John C. Power

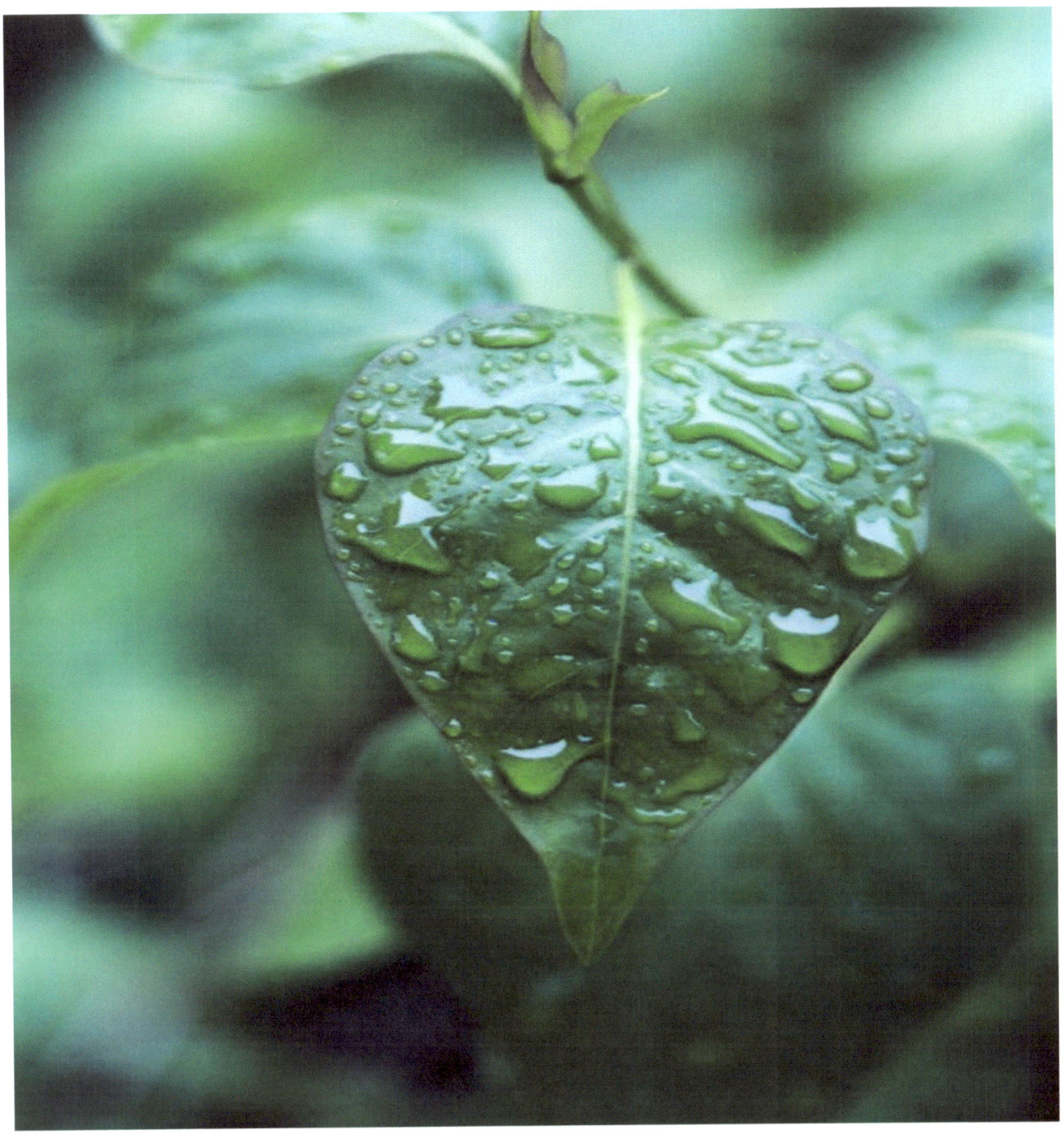

After an early morning shower, the rain leaves behind its own creative image. Normally I stay away from excessive amounts of any one color such as this green but this one was an exception.

'MOUNT SUGARLOAF #1'
South Deerfield, Massachusetts
John C. Power

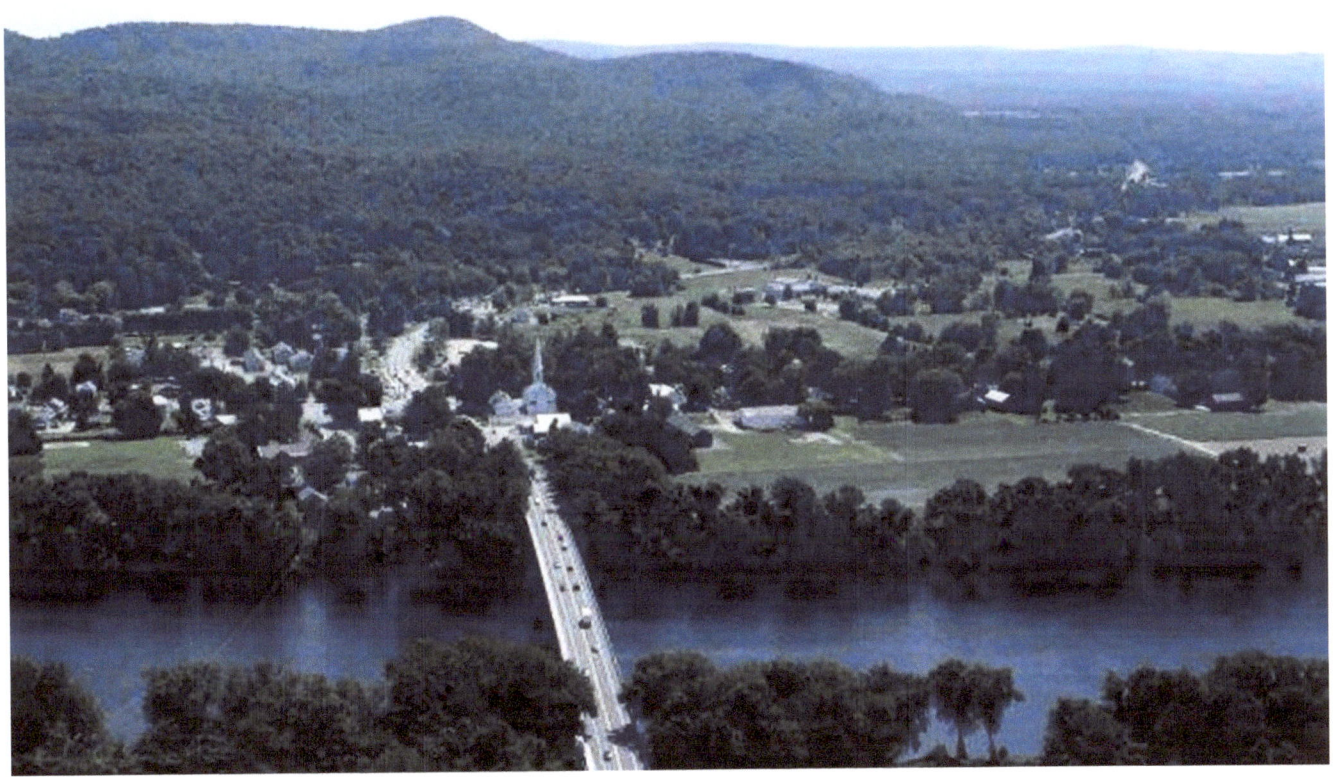

Driving up Mt. Sugarloaf is always fun. Coming down is another story. At the top of this mountain you can see the valley for miles. It's a beautiful local scene.

'OLD BARN'
Hadley, Massachusetts
John C. Power

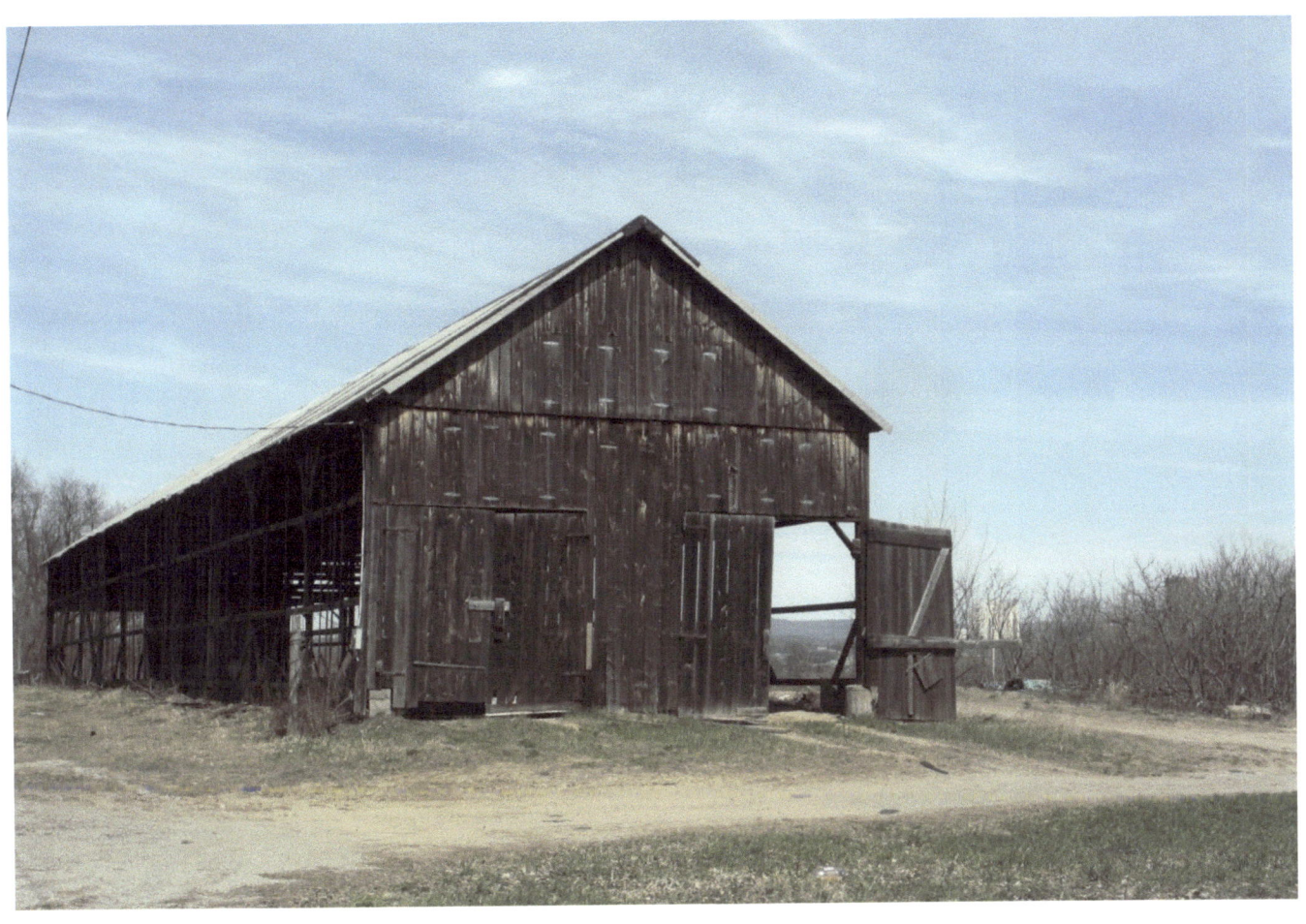

I came across this old tobacco barn one day when I had to make a detour. It's a good thing I had my camera with me. I drove by the same field only a day or two later and it was gone! It must have been taken down.

'ENTRYWAY GATES'
Northampton, Massachusetts
John C. Power

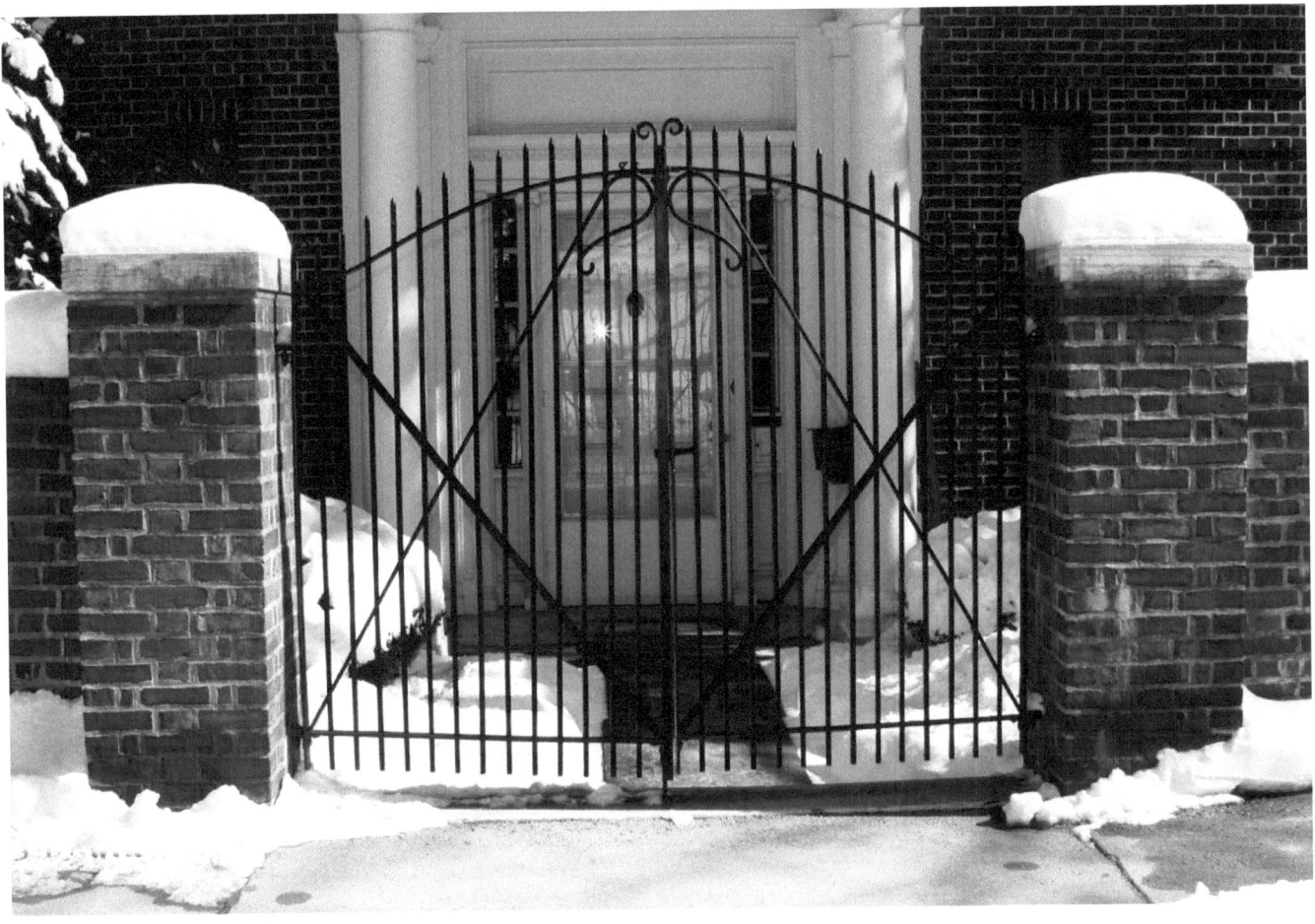

These black iron gates made for an interesting scene after a winter storm in Northampton. Snow is one of the most difficult things to photograph, but the contrast is nice here in black and white.

'SUMMER SUNSET'
Amherst, Massachusetts
John C. Power

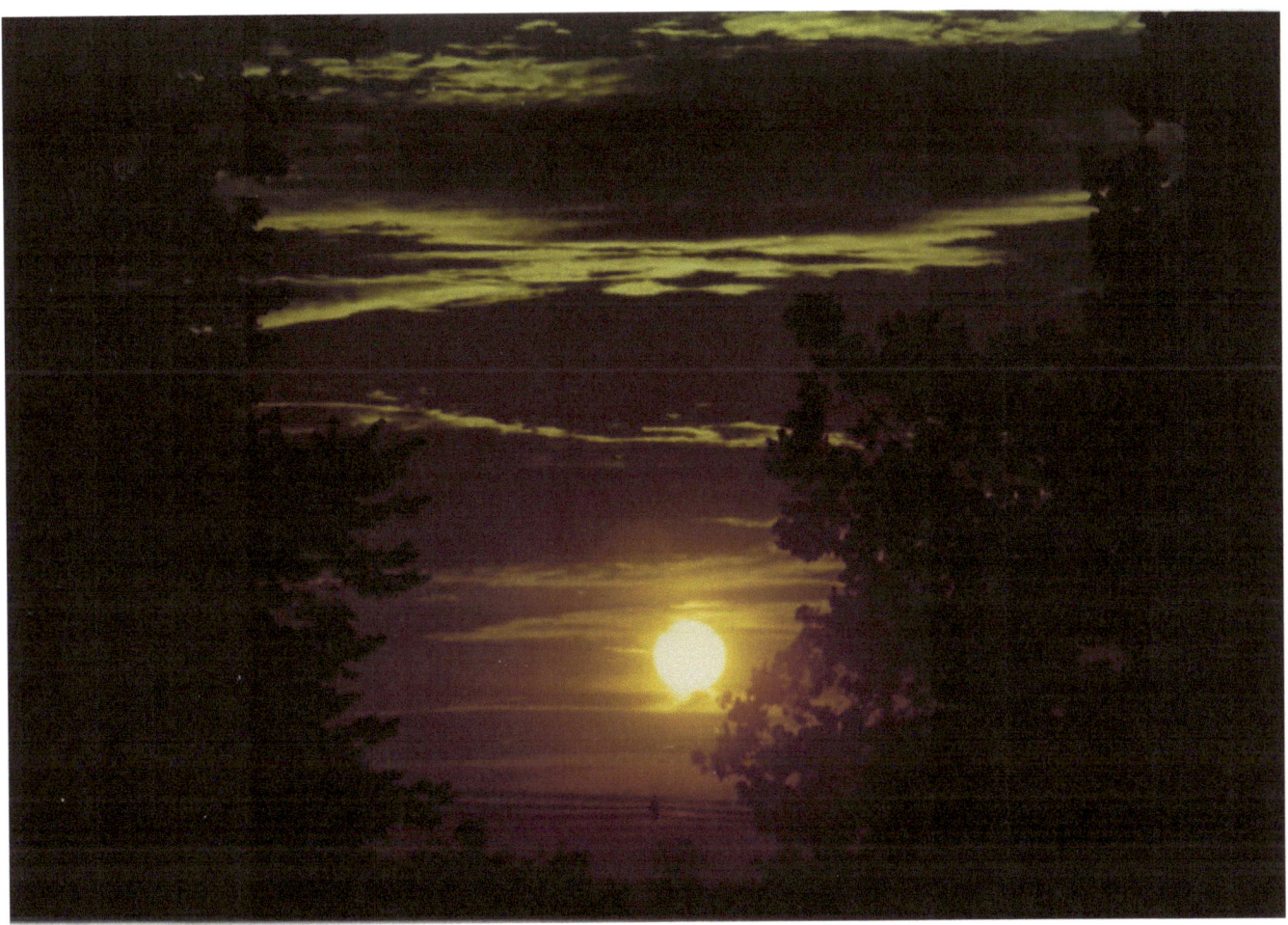

I saw this sunset one evening out my kitchen window. I grabbed my camera and went out to photograph it. This one was a bit of a darkroom experiment in the end. I raised the temperature of the chemicals and increased the time to create a more dramatic effect.

'MOUNT SUGARLOAF #2'
South Deerfield, Massachusetts
John C. Power

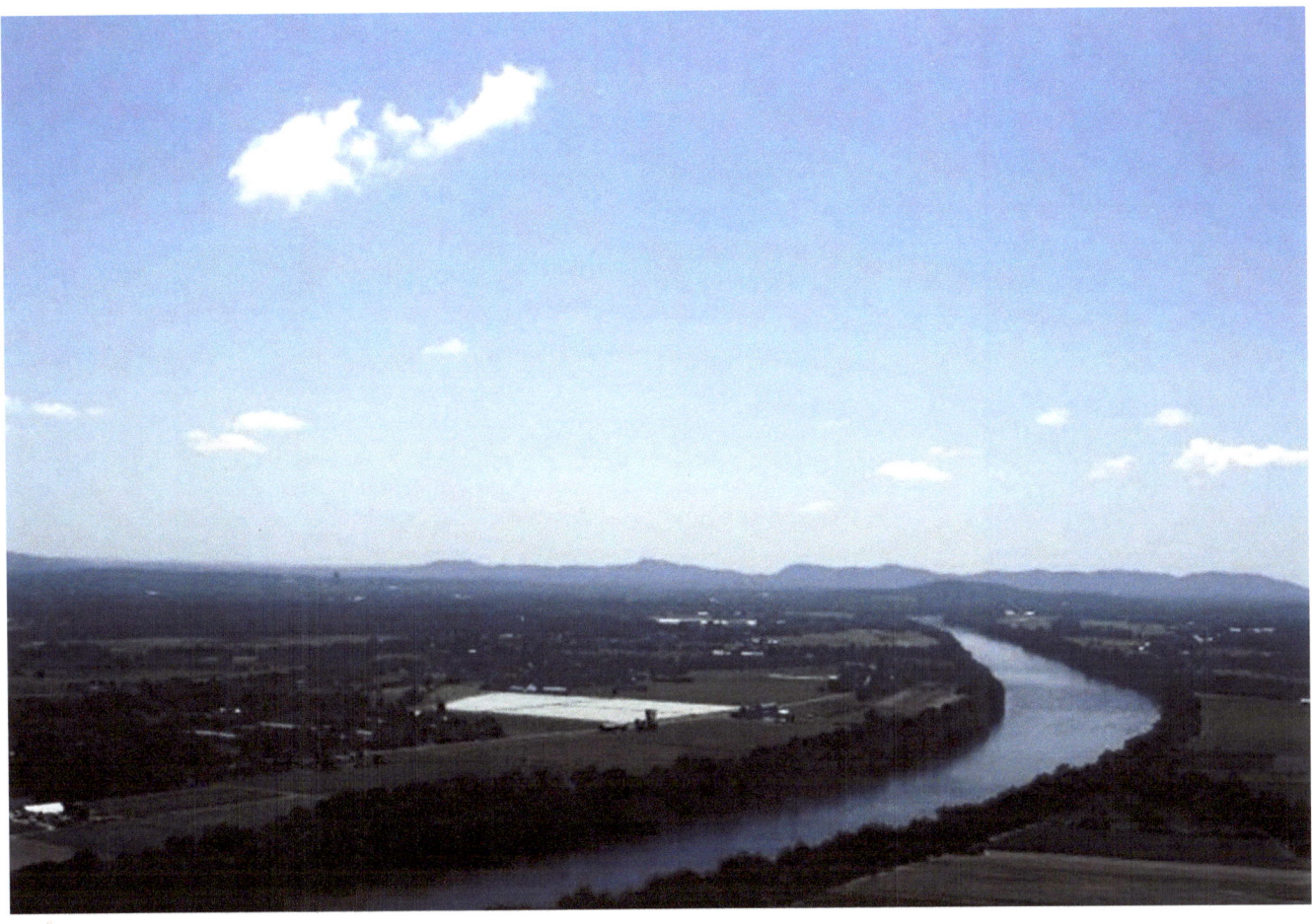

This is another great scene off the top of Mt. Sugarloaf. This time it's from the other side of the mountain. From that height you can really see how the Connecticut River winds around for miles and miles.

'SUN AND TREES'
Amherst, Massachusetts
John C. Power

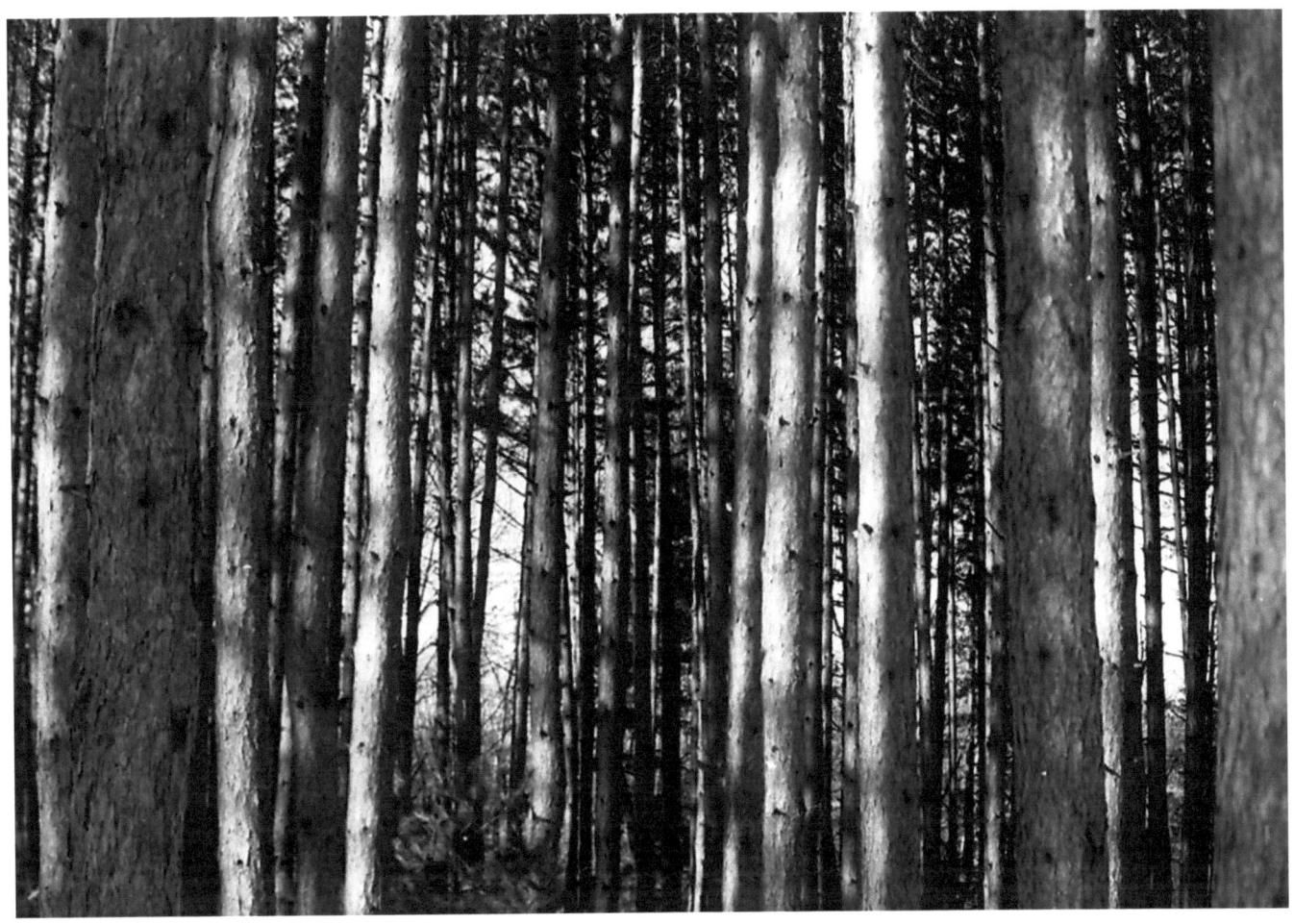

After an unexpected snow storm in April, the sun came out and cast really nice shadows on these trees on a hiking trail. Not long after I took this photograph spring decided to make a return and all the snow melted.

'SPENCER'
My Loyal Friend
At home
Amherst, Massachusetts
John C. Power

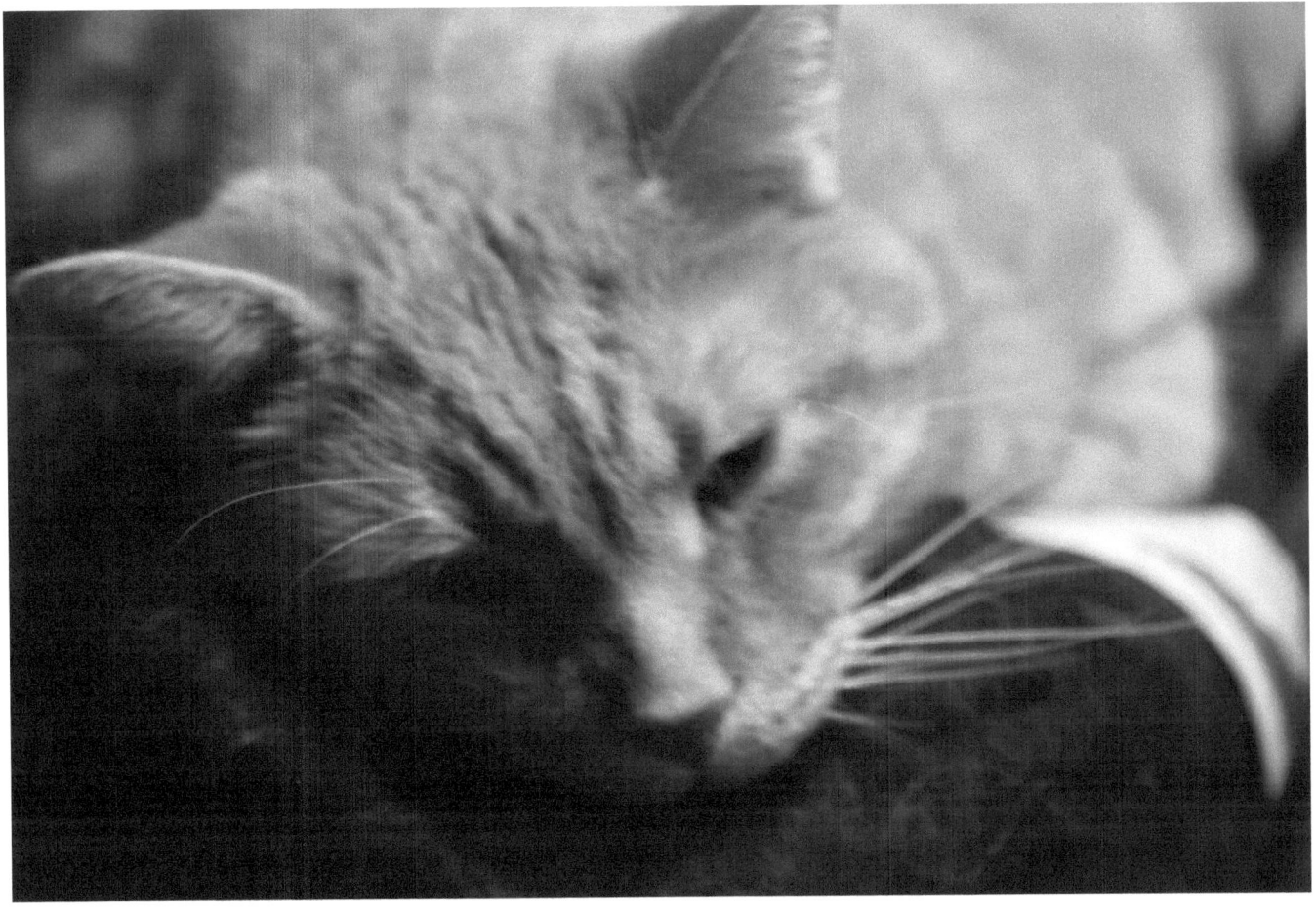

Spencer was an orange tabby cat that found me in the spring of 2002. Here he is caught in black and white with a sepia tone. He passed away not too long ago at the age of sixteen. We have some great memories. I miss him a lot.

'PUFFERS POND WATERFALL'
Amherst, Massachusetts
John C. Power

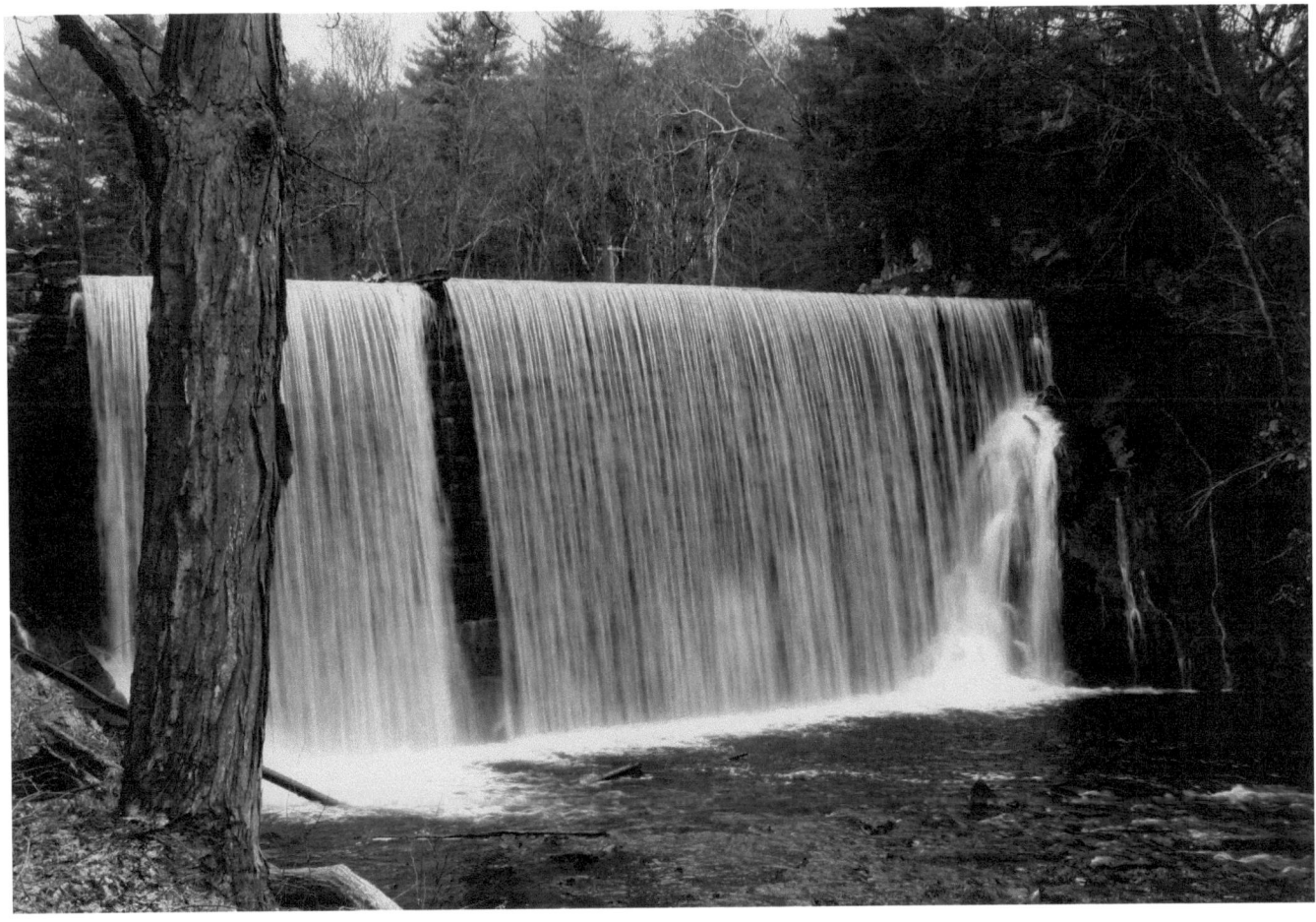

This is the waterfall at Puffers Pond in Amherst. It's a popular spot in the summer time for people to swim and fish. I've shot photos of this waterfall before at different times of the year. I never get bored here because I always find something new.

'BUTTERFLY FACE'
South Deerfield, Massachusetts
John C. Power

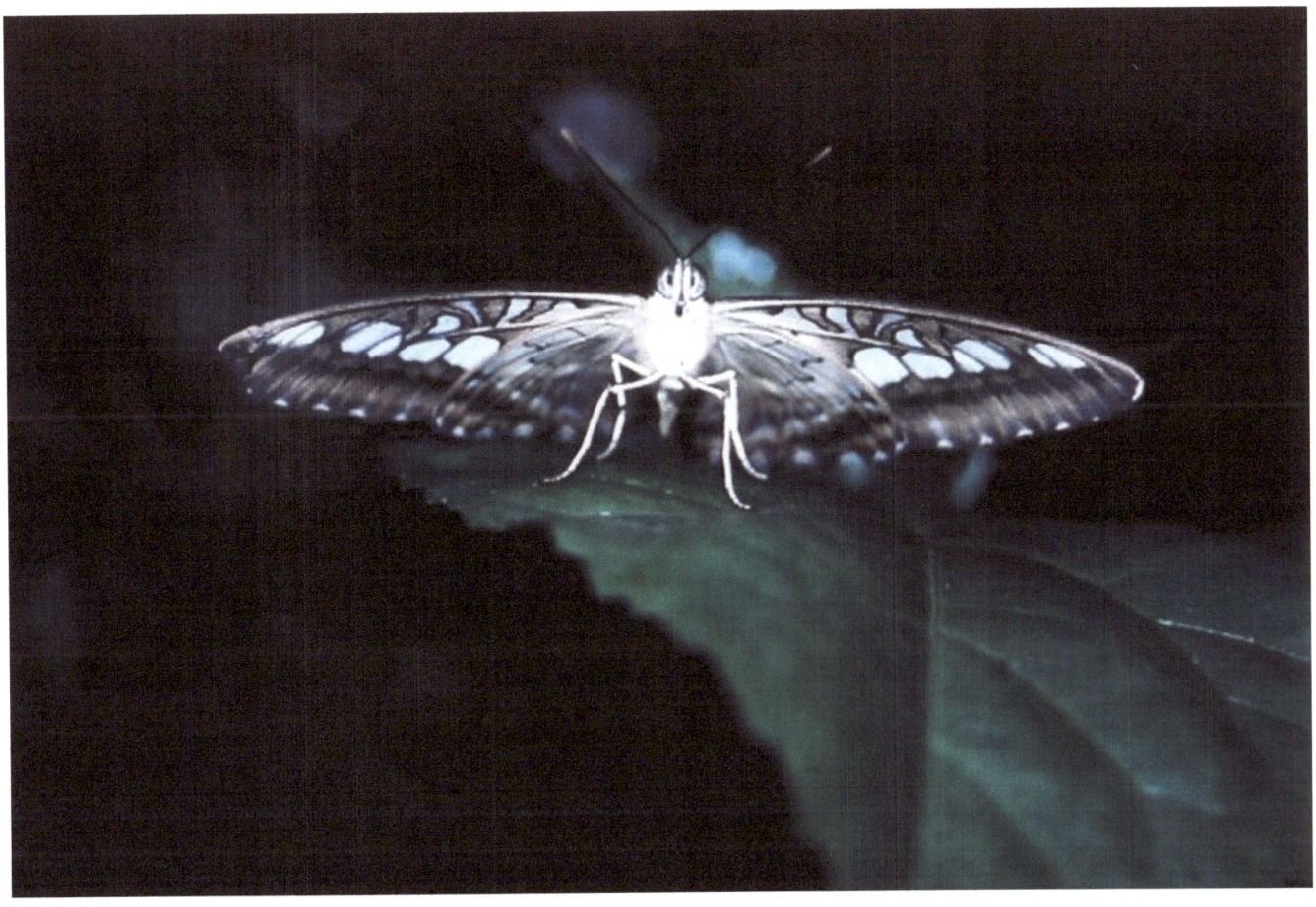

This is an interesting photo to say the least. You can actually see the facial features of this butterfly as it looks into the camera. Many people have purchased this one from me and it still gets talked about a lot.

'COKE CANS'
At Home
Amherst, Massachusetts
John C. Power

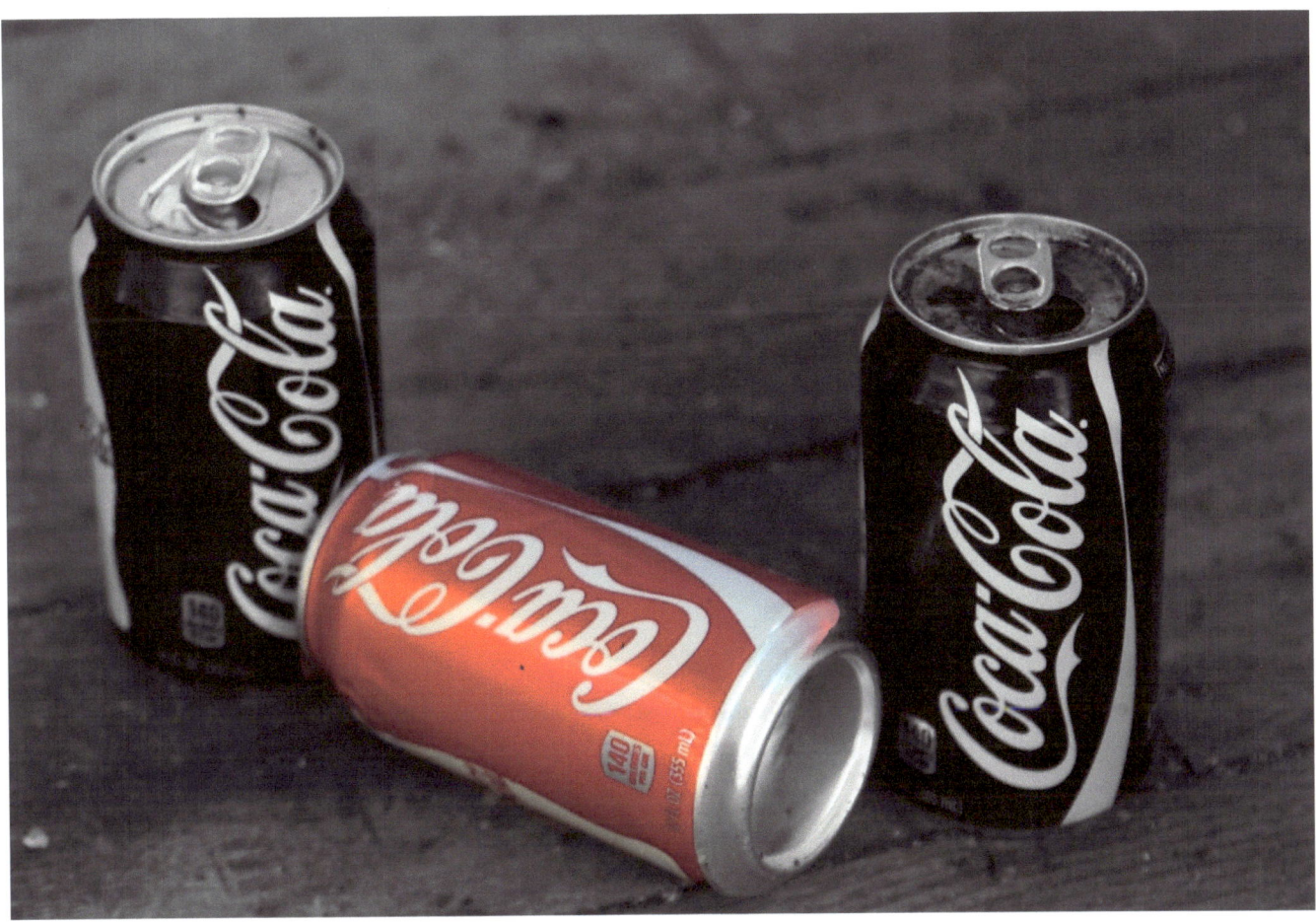

I know I've done quite a bit of color as well as black and white photographs. I figured mine as well mix it up a bit. These cans fell out of the recycling container one morning on the front porch when I got this idea.

'WAGON WHEELS'
Monson, Massachusetts
John C. Power

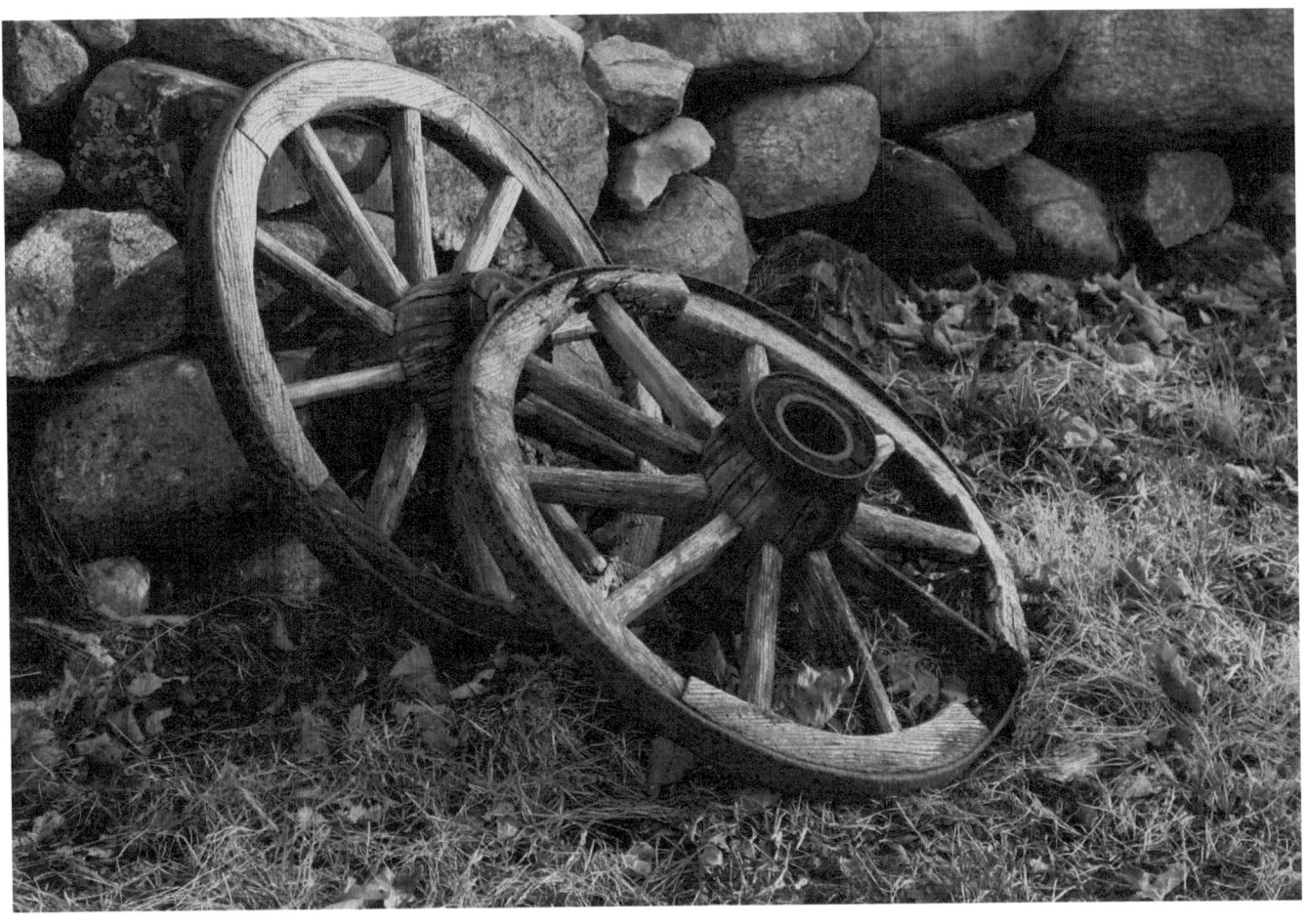

I got a kick out of these old fashioned wagon cart wheels. I especially liked it when I shot it on black and white and added the sepia tone again. I was visiting my sister and her husband in Monson when I came across this unique subject.

‘BLUE STONE STEPS’
Amherst, Massachusetts
John C. Power

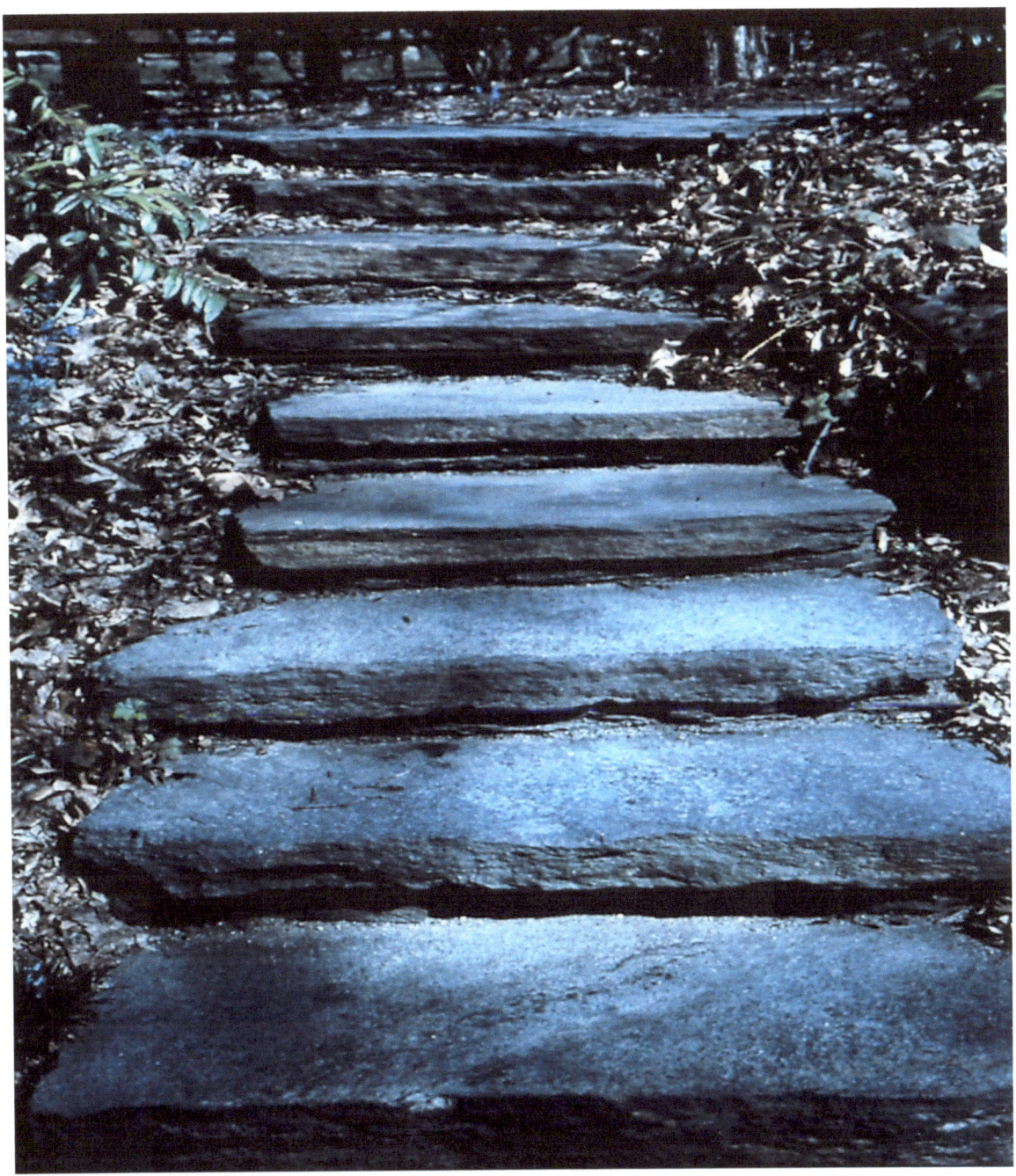

This was another one of those old school darkroom experiments. I was trying to save a roll of slide film that was a good few years past the expiration date. I decided to just guess at the time and temperature during the film processing. These steps were in a memorial garden behind the public library.

'EARLY MORNING FOG'
Easthampton, Massachusetts
John C. Power

The early morning fog made for a nice view over this farm field. The hazy humid air seemed to add to the effect. I'm glad I took this shot when I did because fifteen minutes later the fog started to burn off and clear out.

'RHODODENDRON'
At Home
Amherst, Massachusetts
John C. Power

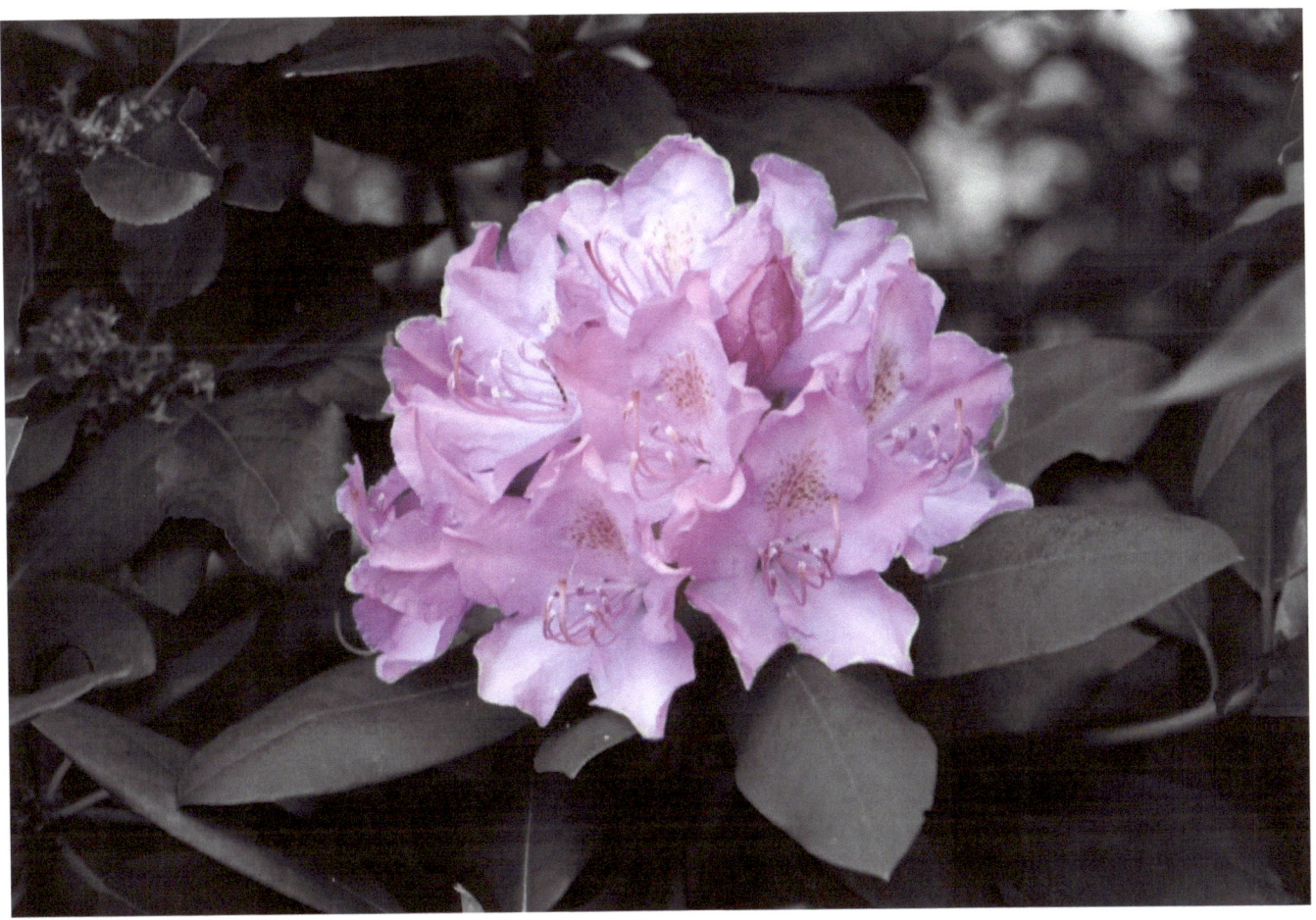

Here is another black and white with color mix. The rhododendron was in full bloom at this time of year. If this shrub could talk I wonder if it might say it felt out of place.